Reclaiming the "V" Word

Other books in the Lutheran Voices series

LUTHERAN

VOICES

Reclaiming the "V" Word
Renewing Life
at Its Vocational Core

Dave Daubert and Tana Kjos

Augsburg Fortress

Minneapolis

Library of Congress Cataloging-in-Publication Data

Daubert, Dave, 1960–
    Reclaiming the "V" word : renewing life at its vocational core / Dave Daubert and Tana Kjos.
        p. cm. — (Lutheran voices)
    Includes bibliographical references and index.
    ISBN 978-0-8066-7057-7 (alk. paper)
    1. Vocation—Christianity. I. Kjos, Tana. II. Title.
    BV4740.D34 2009
    248.4—dc22
                                2009015459

13 12 11 10 09   1 2 3 4 5 6 7 8 9 10

To Emma, Erin, Kirsten, Nathan, & Ethan
Be who you are—it is enough
See what you have—it is abundant
Do what matters—it can change the world

Contents

Foreword

"Zacchaeus, hurry and come down; for I must stay at your house today" (Luke 19:5).

Sam is the kind of guy you'd love to go out for a beer with (even if the strongest thing you drink is a black cup of Joe). He's one of the good guys. You know what I mean? You can tell he can be focused, even driven, when he needs to be but he has an easy-going way about him. He's kind-hearted. He tries to do the right thing by his family and at work. He's smart, too. I don't think there's a single subject he couldn't have a conversation with you about and at least sort of know what he's talking about but without sounding like a smarty-pants. You'd never know that he is one of the most powerful people in the town where he lives. He's as unpretentious as a person could be. In fact, he'd probably want to disagree with me about just how influential he is!

But over the years Sam has advanced professionally into a position that now gives him enormous responsibility. The decisions he makes everyday impact the lives of countless people, their businesses, schools, and neighborhoods. With a single word he influences who gets noticed, what issues become important, and what challenges get tackled. I was a little stunned, therefore, when I heard Sam tell a small group of people at his church a few months back that he's been doing some real soul searching lately.

"I'm looking back over the last twenty-five years of my life," Sam said quietly but with the kind of raw emotion that both got our attention and made us want to look away, "and I'm thinking *what was the point?*"

This book is for Sam and for anybody else out there taking stock of your life and wondering the same thing. If you're not sure what the point of your life is, the authors of this book will help you find it.

For going on a decade now I've been trying to help reclaim some important words that have been misunderstood or so taken for granted that they have become almost useless. That effort has produced a series of books: *Reclaiming the "L" Word* (2003) tells how one congregation articulated its own particular set of guiding principles. But the real point was to articulate in a simple, clear, and compelling way what it means to be a Christian who happens to be Lutheran for the sake of recovering our identity, confidence, and sense of common purpose. *Reclaiming the "C" Word* (2006) attempts to deconstruct clericalism, institutionalism, and various other unhelpful ways we have of thinking about and doing church together in order to recover a definition of church that begins with *people* who have been called by Christ and empowered by the Holy Spirit to participate in God's mission to love, bless, and save the world. *Reclaiming the "E" Word* (2008) is, first, a challenge to embrace our identity as evangelical people who have been given the *really* Good News of God's radical and unconditional love to share and, second, an invitation to learn from congregations that have a proven track record of connecting with their neighbors in a meaningful and powerful way.

One thing each of these books has in common is a core belief that God is up to something big and wonderful in this world and that our job is to be as helpful to God as we can. All three of these books make the case that each one of us is invited to be a part of what God is up to in our everyday lives, that we are called, in fact, to "be the church both whenever we gather *and wherever we go.*" They have, I think (I hope!), helped people reflect on what it means to be the church where they work, live, and play. But, finally, each of these books has had as their primary agenda helping *congregations* become more vital for the sake of God's mission.

Dave Daubert and Tana Kjos care about your congregation, too. And because they believe that *changed people change church*es they'll be surprised if what happens in your life doesn't, in some way, transform the faith community you love.

But I'm giving you fair warning here: These authors aren't going to be satisfied to meet up with you over the coffee pot after Sunday morning worship.

They're coming to your house for dinner.

They're going to tag along with you to work tomorrow. They're going to be in the bleachers while you coach your kid's Little League team and waiting outside the booth while you cast your vote. Wherever you go and whatever in the world you're doing, the questions they ask will go with you: What is God's purpose for me here? What gifts, assets, and passions have I been given to put into the service of God's loving mission? What is God already doing here that I can jump in and be a part of? What is breaking God's heart—right here where I live, work, and play—that ought to be breaking mine, too?

What is God doing here . . . and how can I help?

That is the missional question that ought to be at the center of our life together, as church. But it is also—or ought to be, anyway—the central question of the Christian life . . . of my life . . . and yours. It is in asking that question, everyday in every single circumstance, that reclaiming the "V" word begins.

About a month after Sam confessed that he fears he may be living a pointless life, he told me about what he described as the worst week he's ever had. Huge changes in his field have meant layoffs, reorganization, and "retraining." People who have a lifetime of experience—including Sam—have suddenly found themselves having to reapply for their jobs. That week was exam week. If you failed, you were fired. If you passed, you may have a shot at keeping your job. Sam finished the exam early. Realizing that, in fact, the exam wasn't even all that hard, Sam knew the biggest obstacle they were all facing was their own fear and anxiety. So Sam did something his higher-ups would never have approved of. He went around the room quietly encouraging each test-taker.

"It's not that hard," he said. "Just try to stay calm."

"Come on," he encouraged. "You know this stuff."

"Keep breathing! It'll be okay."

I told Sam how blessed those people were to have him in the room that day.

"I was just trying to think about what Jesus would do," he said.

"Jesus *did* do something," I said. "Jesus was right there in that room, telling everybody it'd be okay."

Sam looked a little puzzled.

"Jesus," I said, "was doing it through *you*."

There's no question that God does some pretty amazing stuff in and through our congregations. But it is no more amazing than what God does—and wants to be doing—in and through you out there where you work and play and live. Reclaiming the "V" word is about learning to have eyes to see what God is up to wherever in the world you find yourself . . . and daring to jump in to help. It is about learning that, in fact, *that* is the whole point.

Kelly A. Fryer

1

The "V" Word Dilemma

As we write this book, it's hard to miss the headlines announcing more layoffs almost every day. Even corporations who survived past economic downturns without major job cuts are shedding employees at an astonishing pace today. We know friends, neighbors, and family members who have lost their jobs. Maybe you too have been laid off. That's the situation our friend Tracye found herself in not long ago.

Tracye had spent most of her adult life working in corporate America. In fact, she worked for the same corporation for twenty-five years. That's a long time to give to anything, let alone a job. Tracye could easily have been angry when she was let go after all those years. Instead she seized the opportunity in a time of transition to ask herself questions about what she loved and what gave her energy. Questions like: What gifts do I have to share? What passions do I want to engage? Then she took a good look at her community, a place that she cares about deeply, and asked: What does this place need? How can I make a difference here? In the end, Tracye responded to what she learned about herself and her community by leaving corporate America altogether and opening a great little wine shop that caters to people who are as diverse and complex as the wines she serves. Tracye opened a place dedicated to what she knows—wines and hospitality—and what she loves—people, laughter, and community.

Tracye's shop is a place where people get to know one another, often over impromptu games of UNO. It's a place where friends introduce one another to new friends, and community grows. It's a place that encourages and enables building bridges, not walls, between people. On the evening of the 2008 presidential election we gathered at Tracye's shop with people of different races, political views, and economic means to witness history being made. It was an amazing night. But that's not unusual. Every night in Tracye's shop is special because Tracye has found her calling. Instead of being angry about losing a job, Tracye chose to reclaim a sense of vocation.

How Did We Get Where We Are?

Our work has taken us all over this country, and no matter where we go we encounter people who are confused about vocation. It is apparent to us that many people have forgotten who they are. They have forgotten how to do what matters most to themselves and to others. As a result, many people hate their jobs, even though they can't imagine an identity apart from their work. People have let their jobs define their lives, leading many to feel used up instead of useful.

The fact that *The Purpose Driven Life*[1] by Rick Warren is one of the bestselling books of our time is evidence that we are hungry for our lives to have meaning, to know that who we are and what we do matters. This hunger is increasing daily, especially among baby boomers transitioning from careers to retirement. On the other end of the spectrum, the Millennial Generation (those born between 1980 and 2000) see meaning and purpose as central for their lives both inside and outside of the workplace. They aren't interested in marking time, but in making their mark on the things they value by getting involved in environmental, economic, and political issues. This generation isn't content to simply be employed. They want to know that there's *a reason* for what they do that goes beyond a paycheck.

The truth is, we all yearn to discover our calling as Tracye has discovered hers. The other truth is that God is at work in the world and wants our participation. God is up to amazing things in and through us, whether we realize it or not. When we fail to see God's activity in our lives, we end up discouraged. Lacking a sense of vocation, life seems meaningless and empty. It is time to reclaim the "V" word so that we can jump on board with what God is doing in our lives and in our world with more intentionality and enthusiasm. We all have a purpose. We each have callings. How we take up the call to vocation—to be useful to God in all that we do—will shape who we are and what we do in ways that may surprise us.

The first step to reclaiming a sense of vocation in our lives is to understand how we got to where we are in the first place. The fact is that we have fallen victim to three deeply ingrained misunderstandings about the relationship between what we do and who we are. We call these the traps of occupation, religious work, and avocation.

The Trap of Occupation

Since the industrial revolution, Americans have come to define ourselves less and less by who we are and more and more by what we produce. Children are encouraged at an early age to begin thinking about what they want to be when they grow up. Societal norms are such that we think if we aren't paid for what we do then we don't really work. Take for instance the stay-at-home mom who says, "I don't work. I'm just a mom." We have a problem with how we understand occupation, and it is a big obstacle to reclaiming a sense of vocation.

Consider Phil, a guy we met who worked in a factory until it closed a little more than a year ago. When asked, "What do you do during the week?" he replied, "Nothing." Pressed a little further Phil admitted that he was trying to fix up his house while he looked for a job. He also volunteers to do projects at his church and through ministries his church sponsors. Phil wasn't spending his days sitting on the sofa, watching television. But because he wasn't holding down a paying job, he believed he did "nothing." The implication? If I lack a paid occupation then I do nothing. In fact some would say I *am* nothing.

On the other hand, there are productively employed people who feel they are missing out on what they are truly called to do. Catherine worked for a time in an agency that advocated for and monitored early childhood development programs. She received excellent pay and benefits for her work and believed that what she was doing was important, but when asked if she had liked the work she replied, "No, I hated every day of it for the whole time I was there. I was too far from the source." It was important for Catherine to use her gifts to do something that she felt passionate about doing.

In his book, *To Know As We Are Known*[2], Parker Palmer describes how we tend to live one-eyed lives. By this he means that we spend most of our time looking through the lens of the mind while neglecting the eye of the heart. Consequently we live partially blind. This insight is helpful in understanding the confusion about our vocation. Through our mind's eye it makes good sense to stay in a job that we don't like because we have bills to pay, a family to support, and needs to meet. The problem is that making life decisions based on the bottom line can keep us from seeing the impact our unhappiness has on the environment in which we work, on our employers and co-workers and the public we serve, and even on the people closest to us outside of the workplace. We are blind to the fact that we choose to do things that benefit a few while others suffer greatly. Palmer would argue that looking with the eye of the heart *and* the eye of the mind would help us see the whole picture much better. Then we would know that because we *can* do something doesn't mean we *must* or even that we *should*.

The Trap of Religious Work

A second misconception is that the call to religious work is often seen as a higher calling than the secular occupations in which most people are employed. We can trace the beginning of this notion back to the fourth century when Constantine, the first Christian emperor of the Roman Empire, made Christianity the "preferred" religion of the empire.

Until then Christians often risked being put to death if they were discovered to be followers of Jesus and adherents to a religion that was outlawed by Rome. By legalizing Christianity, Constantine made it possible for Christians to worship freely and openly. That's a good thing, right? Well, yes, but it also meant that practicing one's faith didn't demand quite the same courage and commitment that it had when being Christian considerably upped the chances of dying a martyr's death. As "normal" Christianity became more complacent with regard to discipleship, some Christians adopted lives of self-denial in devotion to Jesus, who gave up his life for them. In some cases this led to the development of monasteries and convents, where Christians lived celibate lives with little or no personal property and where days were ordered around prayer, worship, humble work, and acts of mercy. In time, religious orders came to be understood as a Christian's highest calling.

Even Martin Luther fell for this trap—for a while. Caught in a horrific lightning storm, a terrified Luther fell to the ground and reportedly cried out, "Help, St. Ann! I will become a monk!" In other words, if Luther's life were spared, he would give up his plan to become a lawyer and aspire to the higher calling of the priest-hood. Luther survived the storm and kept his promise, but after a few years he came to understand that that there aren't greater or lesser calls. Luther argued that we are called to honor God and serve our neighbor in our particular situations, and to support his argument he held up the image in Romans 12 and 1 Corinthians 12 of a single body made up of many members. Luther left the monastery, married, and had children. But as his situation changed, his commitment to honoring God by serving God's people never wavered. In doing so, Luther sent the message that you need not be a religious professional to be serious about your faith and your life's work.

But old understandings don't die easily. Centuries after Luther's influential writing on vocation, the work of priests, pastors, and ministers continued (and often continues) to be seen as more special than work done in the secular arena. To be a church worker is seen as a "high calling," and for many, to be a pastor is to be seen as having received the highest calling of all. Perhaps language is part of the problem. Have you noticed? We *hire* people in every segment of the work force except church professionals. Pastors and priests are *called*. What are the implications of such language? On the one hand, some feel dismissed and less unimportant, while on the other hand, some feel more pressure than is reasonable. Everyone is captive in some way to a false sense of vocation, where what you do in life matters more than the fact that *you are useful to God in whatever you do*!

Reclaiming a vibrant sense of vocation, understood as God's gift to each and every one of us, frees laypersons and pastors alike to live missional lives. The particulars of God's call vary from one individual to the next, but part and parcel of every call are ample opportunities to love and serve our neighbor and therein participate in what God is up to in the world. Perhaps you have seen a sign as you leave some church buildings that says, "You are now the mission field." This is a helpful reminder that the world, not just the church, is the object of God's love.

The Trap of Avocation

There is a tendency in American culture—even American religious culture—to equate vocation with occupation, meaning the work that takes up the majority of our time and energy. Everything else, including but not limited to community service, hobbies, jobs we do on the side, caring for family, nurturing friendships, volunteering, working for causes, gets lumped into a category called avocation. Given this mindset, we are tempted to believe that we can work at our occupations to pay the bills and turn to our avocations to live out our callings. But there is a problem with relegating our callings to our spare time. Most of us have precious little time to spare, and at the end of busy workdays we are exhausted and have little energy to give to the pursuits that matter to us most. So, rather than feeling fulfilled through our avocations, we are overcome with guilt and an increased sense that our lives lack meaning and purpose.

This contributes to a whole other level of stress in already stressful lives. How do we cope? We schedule days at the spa to work out knots. We indulge in retail and travel therapy. We turn to prescription drugs at rates that exceed anywhere else on the globe. And we look forward to retirement, when we believe we will finally have the time, the energy, and the focus to find fulfillment in our lives.

True, we sometimes find time and energy to do what we think of as more significant things. Busy people serve in soup kitchens, build houses with Habitat for Humanity, walk to raise money and awareness for breast cancer research, and do all sorts of other amazing things. But compartmentalizing "God's work" to one part of our lives and not another isn't healthy; nor is it possible. Reclaiming the "V" word is not about finding time and energy for making grandiose differences in the lives of others—though such ventures are certainly part of God's call—as much as it is about recognizing that we fulfill God's call in loving our spouse, caring for our children, talking to our next-door neighbor, doing our best in our daily work, being attentive to our co-workers, and making choices countless times each day to act with justice, kindness, and humility toward others. Because God is mixed up in all of life—our occupations, our noble avocations, our relationships (and all that we do)—everything becomes part of the vocation to which we are called. Only when we get over the idea that some acts matter to God and others don't will we find the truth: all of life matters to God.

We Have Some Work to Do

We may not love what we do for a living, but we have opportunities where we work to respond to God's call in our lives. Though it may be convenient to think that pastors have calls but everyone else has jobs, God wants us to participate in ministry inside our faith communities and in our neighborhoods, in our workplaces and in our families. We may dream of one day starting a free daycare center in a run-down, inner city neighborhood or an elementary school in an impoverished country (and those are wonderful dreams!), but there's no ignoring the fact that God is at work and God's call is upon us here and now. What are we waiting for? Let's not waste another minute!

For Reflection and Discussion

1. Read Genesis 1:1-2:4a. As you read it, how do you think God felt as each day unfolded and creation was formed? Thank about the people who have lived and worked with God's world throughout history. With what aspects of human involvement do you think God is most pleased? What things about how people have used creation make God sad?

2. Think back over your lifetime. What was the worst job you ever had? What was the best job you ever had? As you compare them, what made them different? What can you learn from thinking about them?

3. What do you most enjoy doing? How could you find more ways to do that activity in your life? Is there a way you could do that in order to use it for something useful that was also fun for you?

Prayer

Dear God, we know that all things were made through your work, and as you looked at what you made, you smiled, for it was good. Help us to find things we do to be meaningful, productive, and helpful—and may we smile at the fruits of our labor as well. In Jesus' name we pray. Amen

2

What Is God Doing and How Can We Help?

The gospel—God's good news for us in Jesus Christ—is that God is deeply committed to participating in our lives and in the life of the world. This is a relational commitment from a Trinitarian God who has been living together in a committed relationship as Creator, Redeemer, and Holy Spirit since before the beginning of time. But it is also a physical commitment from a God who comes in the flesh and lives right in the middle of all this stuff—even willingly getting hurt by the toxic mess we humans have made of life.

Why would God do this? In *Living Lutheran*,[1] Dave shared the story of a late night phone conversation he had with his father that wrestled with religion and its connection to God and life. During the course of the conversation, they talked about many issues having to do with faith and life, but the center of the discussion was the petition from the Lord's Prayer, "thy kingdom come, thy will be done, on earth is it is in heaven." Every week, Christians of all ideologies and political backgrounds pray that God will change the world, draw it forward, and fulfill the dream that God has. Jesus taught us to pray for it and he taught us to pray for it before we ask for anything else!

This petition about the coming of God's kingdom on earth lies at the heart of the Lord's Prayer, and the things that follow are like bullet points: life's necessities, reconciled relationships, good choices, setting people free from the evil that holds them captive. They are little pieces of earth being transformed to look like heaven, as the Celtic saying asserts, "As above—so below." Every time this happens, in the midst of the happening, we glimpse the kingdom of God—if only for only a moment. But in the glimpse we see God's dream breaking in around us. God is on the loose, moving among us to bring about God's kingdom here and now. And God is working around the clock to help people not only to see, but also to be a part of what is happening right now. God is not only working at this all the time, God is also using people all over to help get it done!

Recently we led an event for congregational leaders to help them renew their congregations. At the event, we talked about the Lord's Prayer and how Jesus taught us to pray for God's dream and then to watch and work for it to break into our lives. After the large group session, Kay came up and shared her story. "I started to pray the first line of the St. Francis Prayer every day for the last year," she said. "You know, 'Lord, make me an instrument of your peace.'" Then she proceeded to relate how praying that had changed everything about her life for the past year. "Today, looking at the Lord's Prayer this way has been like a little light turning on for me," she said. "The peace I've been praying for is more than an end to war, I know that. But now I see it is all of this that's in the Lord's Prayer—food and shelter, relationships, our choices, freedom—everything!" Praying for what God wants opens us up to be a part of God's life-changing action. When people catch a vision for God's dream, they want to help. That's reclaiming the "V" word.

God Prefers to Work in Teams

More and more, it becomes clearer to us that God enjoys working in teams. We know that God could do it all alone, but it's not in God's nature to do alone what God could do with others. God reserves working alone for those times when no one else can be involved (and we are hard pressed to find many examples of this!). Throughout the Bible, we see time and again how God chose people to serve as agents of action and change. And today, God continues to choose ordinary people like us to carry out much of God's work. We help build pieces and glimpses of the world that God promises is on the way. This is critical to understand: God is on a mission to bless and save the world. It is God's mission; it doesn't belong to us. But when we participate in God's mission, we discover that we are useful to God and can make an incredible difference in the world that God loves. Because God has a mission, we discover that we have a purpose.

Recognizing that we are caught up in God's mission makes a difference in how we understand the church. The church is no longer an end in itself but a means to an end. It is one of the vehicles God uses and through which God works. We believe that renewing the church can't happen without setting people free to be more intentionally and joyfully involved in what God is up to. God's dream becomes the point, and the life and work of the church and its people take on a whole new look. Reclaiming the "V" word is about that new look.

In *Reclaiming the "E" Word*[2] Kelly Fryer showed the results of research in vibrant larger congregations. A common pattern was that a healthy church helps equip people for this new life. In those communities, people know they have a purpose. Until we set people free from the chains that constrain them and keep them trapped, the church will never fulfill its role in God's mission. But the goal has to be changed from "fix the church" to "be a part of what God is up to." And it is only when people are freed to see and get involved with what God is up to that the church will rediscover its own source of life—dynamic people who are excited about how God is using them!

The theologian Dietrich Bonhoeffer wrestled with this as he tried to decide how to be a faithful disciple in the midst of Hitler's Germany. Like Luther, he concluded that isolating himself from the issues of the world wouldn't make God happy. God was on the loose in the world and wanted Bonhoeffer to be out there, too. In a letter to his brother Karl, Bonhoeffer wrote, ". . . the restoration of the church will surely come only from a new type of monasticism which has nothing in common with the old but a complete lack of compromise in a life lived in accordance with the Sermon on the Mount in the discipleship of Christ. I think it is time to gather people together to do this."[3]

Bonhoeffer was writing about a new kind of Christianity that he believed was more in keeping with Jesus' ministry: to be about the kingdom of God out in the world. He believed that rather than retreating from the world, God's people were to be set free and turned loose to engage a world where God was already on the loose and looking for allies! And since God was involved in all aspects of the world that God had made, there was no place and no work that couldn't be connected to the transformation of the world into the world of God's dream. Suddenly, all work was holy again. No callings were higher than others. And all people could be useful to God!

Baptism—You've Been Put on Notice

Bonhoeffer's vision for the church has a lot in common with the writings of Martin Luther, especially his two kingdoms theory, which took very seriously the idea of our being called to participate with God in the world. In Jesus, Luther saw a God who had made the whole world and had come in the flesh to be a part of it. This was all-important to God; nothing was disposable—it was all worth keeping. Luther saw all people as having a role to play in God's economy. Occupation or status did not matter, for God could use people in any of them. In fact, Luther preached that God could use you even if you didn't know it! According to Luther, God uses all sorts of people to keep things going, to make the world function, and to provide care and concern for the people around us. Faith helps people to *see* their lives as useful to God. Faith allows people to more *intentional* about being useful to God. But Christians do not have a corner on being useful to God. God was (and is) using all sorts of people from all sorts of worldviews.

At the same time, Luther believed that if you did know that God was using you, then that put you in a different place. Luther taught that in baptism God has announced a claim on our lives. Marked with the cross of Christ, we are declared an extension of the work of Jesus and called to remember daily that God had claimed us and is with us in all things. In the baptismal liturgy a promise is made to the baptized that we have been united with Christ—we are never anywhere apart from God. And in the announcement of this good news we are transformed. Not only are we useful like every other human being on the planet. Now we also *know* we are useful!

Consider the words we claim as we affirm our baptisms:

> You have made public profession of your faith. Do you intend to continue in the covenant God made with you in Holy Baptism:
>   to live among God's faithful people,
>   to hear his Word and share in the Lord's Supper,
>   to proclaim the good news of God in Christ through word and deed,
>   to serve all people, following the example of Jesus,
>   and to strive for justice and peace in all the earth?[4]

In baptism we have been put on notice—what we do matters! That means no matter where you find yourself, you are there as an agent of God called to continue the work of pursuing God's dream. That is your vocation! In short, God is on the loose—on a mission to bless and save the world that God both made and loves. And God is using everyone to sustain life and bless others. But if you are a baptized Christian, not only are you useful to God, you have the privilege of knowing it! And that can change everything.

For Reflection and Discussion

1. Read Isaiah 2:2-5. Many passages in scripture give a picture of God's dream for the world. What elements of God's dream in this text touch you most deeply? Do you have favorite scripture images of your own?

2. When you think about God's dream for the world, what images give you the most hope and sense of promise?

3. Where have you seen glimpses of God's dream lately? What is happening in the world that you think makes God smile?

4. Where have you seen things happen that aren't in keeping with God's dream? What is happening in the world that is breaking God's heart?

Prayer

Dear God, we know that the world around us is the world you love. We rejoice at those moments that bring a smile to your face. We mourn the things that break your heart. Use us to be part of the way that you shape your world with love. In Jesus' name we pray. Amen

3

New Eyes for Old Stories

It might sound strange to say it but the problem of our narrow understanding of vocation starts with the Bible. Well, not exactly the Bible itself but with the way we have read and understood so many of the key biblical stories. Reclaiming the "V" word depends on revisiting those stories and listening anew to what God has to say to us through them.

In the Beginning . . .

Let's start right at the very beginning: Can you picture it?

God has spent some time getting things up and running. You have day and night, land, sea, and sky. You have trees and sand, dirt and plants with fruit. There are flowers with wonderful fragrances and bees to pollinate them and humming birds feasting off the pollen. You have dolphins dancing on the water and cows grazing lazily in the newly created fields. It's really paradise! Creation is just lacking one thing—people. And at just the right time, when all is ready, God creates Adam and Eve. Can you imagine their shock, with all of creation at their feet and everything made with them in mind? Imagine the very first conversation between God and the people God has made. We imagine it was rather one-sided. Maybe it went something like this:

"Good morning, people!" (We are pretty sure God got started on these things early.) "I've got some stuff for you to do." (Adam and Eve may have been a bit startled, but that didn't faze God.) "I know at the moment you aren't very busy, just getting started as you are.

So I was thinking: all these things need names." (And so people got to work naming all the other things God had made.)

From the beginning God has asked us to be creative. God has asked us to participate in what God is up to in a way that engages who we are. Our job from the very beginning has been to engage with God and God's creation.

"We bless you," God told the people. "Go fill the earth with all of your goodness. Take care of the fish of the sea and the birds of the air. All of the animals are yours to care for, to protect and use for your needs. Look at the trees with which I have blessed you. I have given you all of this, including the plants that will feed you and yours. Oh, and by the way, don't keep it all to yourself. Go ahead and create. There is plenty as long as you care for it. I have put you here for each other, for those who are not here yet, and for this amazing creation under your feet and above your head."

There was nothing about what God gave Adam and Eve that didn't have to something to do with why God had created them. Their life was created to be about God's amazing work in absolutely every way. Why would we think ours is any different?

If you're thinking, "Okay, that's one story," don't worry, there are lots of others. How about the story of Abram and Sarai? You know, the one where God told a couple of senior citizens to pick up and leave the country where they lived, the place they had called home for a very long time: "Abram, it's God. (Yeah, for real.) I want you to do something for me. I want you to fold up shop, pick up everything you have, and you and Sarai are moving. I have some land for you and a plan."

This time the conversation wasn't so one-sided. "Is that really you?" asked Abram. "Give me a little more to go on. Something my family can wrap their heads around. I mean, come on, I'm seventy-five years old! Now is not exactly the time I was thinking about doing anything but kicking up my feet and enjoying the sunset years!"

"But, Abram that is not what I was thinking at all," replied God. "I have so much in store for you and that amazing woman with whom you have spent your days. I want to bless you with land to call your own—enough for a great nation."

Abram had good reason to be skeptical. Old people with no kids don't have descendants, and to father a whole nation when you hadn't fathered a single offspring was a stretch. Still, Abram did what God asked of him, and he picked up everything and headed for his new home. But even after many years in the new place, Abram and Sarai still had to wait a while longer for the promise. Finally God came back with a new promise, one so radical that Abram and Sarai got new names—Abraham and Sarah. "You are going to be the mother and father of a very great nation," said God.

This, of course, seemed highly unlikely.

But not long after that they got a visit from three men, travelers looking for hospitality. While Sarah went inside to prepare dinner, Abraham and the travelers talked. One of the men told Abraham, "Next year at this time, when I come back, Sarah will have had a son." Back in the tent, Sarah overheard the conversation and laughed to herself, thinking, "I'm way too old for such a thing!"

The truth is, you can never be too old. Or too young. Or too whatever. There isn't a moment in our lives when God doesn't have a purpose for us. God wants us participating in creation in ways we can't even imagine. But just because we don't have an imagination for it yet doesn't mean it won't be so. Be careful about the ideas you laugh at. You never know what God might have in store for you.

New Work for Old Fishermen

The Old Testament is full of stories about God's call on our lives. And so is the New Testament. You might know this one:

There they were at the edge of the sea, nets in hand, sun coming up, when they heard Jesus call. They looked up to see who was speaking to them. What could this man possibly want so early in the morning? Something about him seemed different, even intense. "Hey, what's up?" they cautiously responded.

Maybe Jesus saw how bad the morning on the water had been or maybe he could feel the potential in the early morning moment, or maybe, just maybe he sensed they were hungry for something more. Whatever it was, Jesus saw those fishermen and gave them a challenge, a call to something more. "Come, follow me and I will teach you how to fish for people." And they did, right then and there. They dropped everything for something new.

Now, before we go any further, let's acknowledge that there is a danger in this story—at least the way we have often looked at it. The danger comes when only a part of the story becomes normative. Because most mainline churches are captive to clericalism, there is a real sense that it's somehow special when someone is willing to quit a job to do "real ministry." For instance, an engineer who leaves engineering and goes to seminary earns the accolades of people who admire the willingness to leave behind something secular and answer a "higher calling." Suddenly, people who leave their jobs and become church professionals (especially ordained ones) look like the model we see when the disciples leave their boats and nets to follow Jesus. Serious damage is done—to *both* clergy and to laity—when we assume that this is the norm for true discovery of godly work.

The truth is that this is not the norm for godly work at all. It isn't even the norm for people who are touched by Jesus and sent forth as ambassadors! Look at the story of those fishermen again. Yes, they left their jobs the day Jesus called them, but read *the rest* of the story and you'll be amazed at just how many times those guys ended up back in their boats! It seems like almost every time you turn around in scripture, the disciples and Jesus were back in a boat again! Jesus taught crowds from the shore—in a boat. Jesus calmed the stormy waves and wind and the scared disciples—in a boat! Jesus asked Peter to walk on water, and where was Peter when the challenge came? In a boat! The list goes on and on. It seems that even though they left behind a particular job, the disciples did not leave behind their gifts, talents, and experiences. God used those gifts, talents, and experiences to get the job done!

Take for example the story of Jesus' encounter with the woman at the well from John, chapter 4. Apparently the woman was an outsider in her own town; her reputation was sullied by all sorts of stories from her past—some of her own doing and some where she was taken advantage of by others. Because of her reputation, this woman was forced to wait until no one was around before heading out to the well, thus she came out in the heat of the day, instead of with the others in the morning when things were cool. In his encounter with this woman, Jesus unearthed her story and showed her something about herself and about God. With things as tough as they were for the woman, it might have been really gracious for Jesus to have taken her with him and helped her get a fresh start somewhere else. Instead, transformed by her encounter with Jesus, the woman went *back into town* to tell other people (the same ones she had tried to avoid just thirty minutes earlier) about him. Her transformation and ability to be connected to Jesus' work depended on her *not leaving*! And because of the transformation and the excitement in her, people saw and encountered Jesus for themselves and believed. Had she left to go somewhere else, she may have been almost useless. Only in returning to her own life—*but in a new way that showed God had touched her*—could she really be most useful to God.

The Shepherds of Bethlehem: An Old Job with New Energy

It can be hard to see these familiar Bible stories in new ways after so many years of hearing them read and preached from a particular angle, but it is critical to do so if we are going to be able to understand vocation in a new way. The authors of this book are part of a team of people at A Renewal Enterprise that tries to meet weekly for an hour of Bible study. We connect by phone if need be with members of our team in Illinois and with other team members in Kansas, Pennsylvania, and Winnipeg, Canada. When traveling for work, we can call in for Bible study, too. It's a simple format. Someone picks a text and we read it aloud. Then we ask, "What's going on in this text?" and "What is God up to?" We wait to see what someone observes in the text and then we start to talk about where the lesson takes us. At the end we always ask, "So what do you hear God saying to us today?" As a result of that hour together, we have developed program emphases for our work as a team. Paying attention to what God is saying through scripture can change your life—sometimes really quickly!

Right before Christmas, Jennifer, who lives in the Kansas City area, suggested we read the Christmas story from Luke 2. Now, those of us on the team have heard the story a hundred times (or more!), but we could still learn something new. We talked about how the shepherds, who had one of the lowliest of all jobs in Israel, were the first to get the message and were called to meet the Messiah who had come into the world—also in a lowly place. While the King of kings was being treated like a shepherd, the shepherds were getting the royal treatment from a bunch of angels who came to announce the news. The danger of familiarity is the risk of becoming immune to the text's message—failing to hear a new and living word from God each time we read it. But that day it was like a huge light bulb went off. We realized that when the shepherds were finished checking out Jesus, *they returned to their fields!* They didn't drop their staffs and abandon the sheep to head off to do "real ministry." They didn't march off to seminary or turn away from their everyday lives to work in a far-off mission field. They had a life-changing encounter with God that gave them a new way of seeing, being, and doing *their old lives* in new ways!

Examples like these are repeated again and again in scripture, where we read that people are somehow changed by an encounter with Jesus. In some cases they do try to go with him. But few actually do. More often Jesus *sends* them, changed as they are, *right back to the people and work from which they came*—to be agents of God in their daily lives. It was their life that was changed, and they were sent right back into the context from which they had come! Reclaiming the "V" word usually isn't about leaving your current life to go find a real one. Most often it is about engaging your life with purpose and passion—living your old life in a new way!

In 1 Peter 2:4-10 we read that we are a "royal priesthood" and "God's own people" (verse 9). To be God's people is to have a role in God's work. And it is a role given to *all* of God's people—not just to those who leave their old lives and march off to "do ministry" or "be a missionary" somewhere else. Martin Luther was clear about this, and it is at the heart of the Reformation message. And so, this is important enough to have its own chapter. We'll turn there next to see what Luther had to say as he helped people claim their ministry as God's people—reclaiming the "V" word for themselves!

For Reflection and Discussion

1. The "gospel in a nutshell" is the title often given to John 3:16-17. Read these familiar verses again. What does this passage say about what is most important to God? What lengths has God gone to in order to live that out?

2. God's dream is important enough for God to come in Jesus. How important is God's dream to you? Do you think of it often?

3. How does God want to work through you to advance the dream in your home, job, neighborhood, or congregation? Where have you sensed God using you lately?

Prayer

Gracious God, in Jesus we see how you have come into the world and in scripture we see the lives of people you have used throughout history to do your work. Use us to do your work as well, so that our lives may be useful to you. In Jesus' name we pray. Amen

4

Luther Looks at 1 Peter 2:4-10

Martin Luther wrote many things about a vision of a church where the work of all Christians was viewed as important to God. The shorthand for this is often referred to as "the priesthood of all believers," a phrase that captures Luther's commitment to the calling and ministry of every Christian. It was Luther's contention that the gift of ministry was given by Jesus to *all* of the baptized. It didn't matter to Luther *where* people worked, but it did matter for *whom* they worked—God. And God was (and is) calling all Christians to the vocation of serving their neighbors as agents of God. For Luther, everyone who would act as God's agent was a "priest" and called to do work that shared God's concern for their neighbors. He wrote:

> It would please me very much if this word "priest" were used as commonly as the term "Christians" is applied to us. For priests, the baptized, and Christians are all one and the same. For just as I should not put up with it when those who have been anointed and tonsured want to have exclusive right to the terms "Christians" and "baptized," so I should also not put up with it when they alone want to be called priests. Yet they have monopolized this title. . . . For it must be our aim to restore the little word "priests" to the common use which the little word "Christians" enjoys. For to be a priest does not belong in the category of an external office; it is exclusively the kind of office that has dealings before God.[1]

In this chapter we are going to look at just one of the places where Luther articulated and reflected first on the priestly work of all the baptized. We chose Luther because his work helped start this conversation. But the conversation does not end there. Consider what John Calvin, another important reformer, said on the same topic: "We know that men were created for the express purpose of being employed in labour of various kinds, and that no sacrifice is more pleasing to God, than when every man applies diligently to his own calling, and endeavours to live in such a manner as to contribute to the general advantage."[2] Again we see the sense that God uses everyone's work to shape the world and desires that the work we do make the world a better place. Through our work, God is looking out for our neighbors!

So both Luther and Calvin extended the concept of call, previously used to describe the work of religious professions, to include the work of all people in any and all settings. In the process, they agreed on the simple concept that while the specifics change with each person's talents, personality, and context, ultimately there is a common thread that defines the vocation of all Christians: to be useful to God by serving the neighbor.

An important scripture passage that Luther used to discuss his ideas is from 1 Peter, chapter 2:

> Come to him, a living stone, though rejected by mortals yet chosen and precious in God's sight, and like living stones, let yourselves be built into a spiritual house, to be a holy priesthood, to offer spiritual sacrifices acceptable to God through Jesus Christ. . . . But you are a chosen race, a royal priesthood, a holy nation, God's own people, in order that you may proclaim the mighty acts of him who called you out of darkness into his marvelous light. Once you were not a people, but now you are God's people; once you had not received mercy, but now you have received mercy. (1 Peter 2:4-5, 9-10)

For Luther, the transformation that happens to us in Christ is central. We are transformed from "no people" into "a royal priesthood" and that means that all of us find meaning, purpose, and direction for our lives as we live out our vocations in new ways and with new focus.

Read what Luther says in one part of his commentary on 1 Peter 2:

> Now Christ is the High and Chief Priest anointed by God Himself. He also sacrificed His own body for us, which is the highest function of the priestly office. Then He prayed for us on the cross. In the third place, He also proclaimed the Gospel and taught all men [sic] to know God and Him Himself. These three offices He also gave to all of us. Consequently, since He is the Priest and we are His brothers, all Christians have the authority, the command, and the obligation to preach, to come before God to pray for one another, and to offer themselves as a sacrifice to God.[3]

What Jesus did at the cross was proclaim the good news and pray and sacrifice—*all for the sake of others.* Because we see these present in the life and death of Jesus, we know that they are integral to his own ministry and identity. And when Luther said, "all Christians have the authority, the command, and the obligation to preach, to come before God to pray for one another, and to offer themselves as a sacrifice to God," he made the move from Jesus' ministry to ours.

Proclaim the Good News

Proclamation can take many forms but at its most basic it involves speaking the gospel—sharing it with the neighbor. It involves the use of words. An old adage, often attributed to St. Francis is, "Preach the gospel always. Use words if necessary." There is little evidence that St. Francis said this, nor is there much in the Bible that would point to words as being somehow optional. So while this quote often soothes the conscience of people nervous to share the message, the truth is that the gospel is ultimately a message; it comes as good news. And in a world where fewer and fewer people are using the story of Jesus to interpret their lives, words *are* necessary.

Now this doesn't mean that actions are unimportant (we'll explore this more when we look at sacrifice). Nor does it mean that everyone should be fighting over time in the pulpit (although we believe that more than the ordained ought to spend time there!). But it does mean that all of us need to be able to speak to the hope that is in us and do it effectively, invitingly, and with tact. In other words, we need to be able to name God when we see God at work, and we need to be able to jump on that train, knowing we have the ability to help!

Actions *are* part of the Christian life, but there is nothing about Christianity that gives us a corner on being nice, honest people. There are all sorts of honest, helpful people in the world and most of them are not Christian churchgoers. They may be active in other faith traditions or they may claim no religious ties at all. Words are needed to make the connection, and words can make the case clear that God is bigger than the church and more powerful than our good deeds.

Leaders of faith communities can make more space for people to see God at work in their lives and to practice talking about it. Most "preaching" in daily life is not formally delivered sermons from the pulpit but is situational and on the fly. People need to be familiar with what they bring to the table; they need to have talked about it before they require it in the field so they are be able to access it easily and quickly. Who hasn't had someone come to them in trouble, felt awkward not knowing what to say, and then later thinking, "If only I'd said . . ."?

Few of us are confident at anything significant the first time we try, and if the first time is public, we are even less likely to try at all.

Many of us are still waiting for the first time—having never quite known what to say or how to say it. If people gather each week and never share stories with each other how can we ever think we will know what to do that first time?

Gathering time is storytelling time. Simple practices to encourage storytelling can include a question of the week to discuss and apply sermon themes, turn-to-your-neighbor exercises during the sermon, using table tents or handouts with discussion ideas on them to shape fellowship conversations, and offering classes where students talk as much or more than the teachers. Try really listening to one another, really asking how the week went. Share your observations about God at work in the world. Perhaps you could make it a practice, as you read your local paper or surf the web, to make a mental note of what you think is happening in the world that would make God smile. Also note what you think is making God cry, and share that with someone.

People need to practice seeing God at work in the lives of others *and* in their own lives. We often use examples from scripture to help people think about how God works in people's lives. Once we used the text from Luke 7—a story about a widow whose only son had died—dividing our large group into many groups of three spread out throughout the worship space. One person in each group took on the role of the widow, the crowd at the funeral, or the dead son. We read the story and then each person in the group was given time to talk about how they think their character would feel. There were no experts—just people talking to people. After the groups had had a chance to talk about all three characters, they debriefed and shared their thoughts.

The first time this exercise was done, people talked about the worry and sense of loneliness the widow must have felt when she was left to fend for herself in a culture where having no sons could mean destitution. They also spoke about her joy when the son was raised. Those who were representing the crowd shared a sense of shock and outrage at seeing Jesus interrupt the funeral and touch a dead body in a culture where ritual cleanliness meant you just didn't do things like that.

But with regard to the dead son, they discovered a surprise. The son would awake to find himself in a coffin and ask, "What the heck is going on?" Even though he was the one who Jesus had healed, *he was the only person who didn't know what had happened!* The insight? We often are the last ones to see what God is up to in our own lives. The first step to naming God's action might be to risk saying to someone, "I don't know if you see it this way but I think God is. . . ."

Another simple thing that we can do is change the small talk or banter that is programmed into our culture. Everyone knows that when someone passes you on the street and asks, "How are you?" the appropriate response is "Fine." You could have just been diagnosed with cancer or lost your job, but in many cases the same "fine" response would be easier than unpacking what you were going through. It's safer to say what is expected and move on. But what if we could mix things up a little bit and in doing so also get the attention of people in ways that might make them think a bit?

After thinking about that question, Jeannie began to look at her life and the conversations she had on a daily basis. As someone who worked in a doctor's office she routinely found herself talking to people and the "How are you today?" question would come up— sometimes with dozens of people each day. How could she find a way to reframe the conversation in a helpful way? She eventually decided that instead of "fine" she would say, "richly blessed." As a result, people perked up and she has had many chances to share a helpful word that might not have come if she had settled for "fine."

Prayer

The next of these functions that we will explore is the call to prayer. The gift of Christ's presence in the life of the faithful brings with it an ongoing relationship with God. Through the presence and work of the Holy Spirit, Christians are now able to approach God directly—to intercede with God on behalf of others.

If there is one religious idea that has permeated North American culture it is the concept that everyone has the ability to go directly to God. But many use it as a reason to disconnect from Christian community, saying, "I can go to God for myself. I don't need to go to church to pray." While this is true, it misses the key to priestly ministry—that it is always *on behalf of others*. The call to acknowledge the right of individuals to pray is not meaningful in Luther's thought apart from the question: "Does this express genuine love for my neighbor?"

Leaders need to be challenged with regard to prayer practices. While in many of congregations laity lead the prayers of the people, frequently the closing petition is still led by the ordained minister who often says something like, "Into your hands, O Lord, we commend all for whom we pray. . . ." This subtly communicates that while laity may participate in the prayers, the ratification and summation by clergy is still helpful or even necessary in getting God to really listen. Many congregations now are moving toward having a layperson say the closing petition as well—a healthy practice that communicates a more level playing field in the work of coming before God in prayer.

As we travel around the country we routinely see people who are terrified of praying together. At the end of a meeting we ask, "Would anyone like to close us with prayer?" and the anxiety in the room and peoples' shifting eyes give a clear message—no one wants to! Many lifelong churchgoers who have rarely missed a Sunday are still terrified to lead a prayer. When asked about this, Loretta, a lifelong church member said, "I don't think anyone ever taught us how to pray."

One of the keynote speakers at the ELCA Youth Leaders Gathering in 2005 was Tony Campolo, who shared about his first few weeks as a pastor in Philadelphia. Apparently his language was too plain and didn't measure up to the King James language of the previous pastors, and a woman came to him complaining, "Young man, those are some of the worst prayers that I have ever heard." Campolo reported that he responded to her by saying, "I wasn't talking to you anyway." (He also admitted that incidents like this may be why he ended up teaching college sociology!) Of course, when he told the story, everyone laughed at the punch line. But they also got the point: we pray *on behalf of* people not *to* them. Prayer does not take a special skill—to get started you only need to trust that God is listening and then begin talking. Anyone can do it!

Karen heard Campolo's story and took it to heart. The following weekend at her congregation's annual picnic, Karen got up to lead the group in a table prayer, saying, "I haven't done this before, but I now know that when I pray I'm not talking to you. I'm talking to God. And so I am going to say the prayer today." She proceeded to offer up a prayer that surely made God smile.

Finally, prayer within the context of vocation is not a practice limited to time spent with our faith community. We practice it when we gather so that we can live it when we are apart. It may not be in any official job description, but all who live out their Christian vocations will recognize that they fail to do their work unless they are praying for the people they encounter. For example, teachers who understand their vocation will soon see that praying for fellow teachers, students, and their parents is a part of their work. The same is true of people in any occupation. "Secular" occupations, seen through the lens of the priesthood of all believers, are simply places for Christians to saturate the world with prayer, bringing the concerns of the world before God as well as listening for guidance from God on how best to love our neighbors.

Sacrifice

Living a cross-centered and servant-oriented life is the outcome of being transformed by Christ. The Christian life is more than just the spiritual. The incarnation is all about a God who comes into the world, shares in it even to the point of death, and persists in that love by coming back in the resurrection. This world matters. And that means our work in this world matters to God, too.

Grounded in the cross of Jesus, we are immediately confronted with the reality that the Christian life is a costly calling. Christians are not like everyone else; we are bearers of crosses taken up in a faith that is lived out for the sake of the world and as an expression of our love for the neighbors God has given us. In a few chapters, we are going to discuss the topic of "passions." The word *passion* is derived from the Latin word that means "to suffer." A passion is something you love so deeply that you are willing to suffer for it! Passion is a reason to sacrifice, and that sacrifice is all about love! In fact, all faithful action is lived outwardly in our love of neighbor. While faith directs us toward God, action is directed toward the world. We are called to be instruments of God's love. Therefore, the way we live our lives becomes the vehicle for mission. Mission is not a special emphasis—it is the essence of life itself.

Helen and Maurice lived their whole lives as "ordinary" people. Maurice worked as an airplane mechanic and loved to engineer things. Helen was a stay-at-home mother who never learned to drive a car. On the surface they were the epitome of normal, but underneath they lived an amazing story. They had tithed since the day they were married. To do this they had always lived frugally, keeping their wardrobes simple, driving their cars longer, and doing without a lot of things. Late in their lives they decided they could do more, and in addition to tithing they gave two hundred dollars each month to low income people to buy groceries.

To save money, Helen didn't use a clothes dryer, choosing to hang her laundry on the line to dry. In the summer and on warmer winter days she would hang the clothes outside, and on days colder than twenty degrees she would hang them on racks and lines in the basement. It was a struggle sometimes to do it, but the money she saved would help keep making a difference in the lives of hungry people. That was her vocation and she would sacrifice ease of life in order to live a life that mattered.

People need faith communities that will help them make sacrificial choices. The call to be an alternative to the dominant culture is essential. Even as popular culture encourages people to spend money on all sorts of things they don't need, how can we Christians live lives that waste less and become more generous for the sake of our neighbors? When others assert their rights, can Christians freely give up ours to express care for someone else? When others are too busy, can Christians step forward and give up time to be the agents of God's mission in the world?

Everyday Radicals

The radical nature of the priesthood of all believers is that it honors the daily work of every person. Family, school, jobs, households, neighborhoods are all vehicles for the Christian to live out a faithful life. Even hanging out the laundry matters! God claims us in baptism, declares us to be useful to God, and gives the authority to pray, preach, and sacrifice for everyone, everywhere. God then uses the daily activities we perform as the context for mission. Everyone's work becomes holy and special. In fact, there is no situation where as Christians we have not been called to live out our faith.

Ethics, time management, stewardship, lifestyle choices, use of talents, and all sorts of things are at play here. A healthy ministry will help us live out the priesthood in our vocations by giving us the tools to navigate our situations and make good choices. A healthy ministry will help people ask, "What is Christ calling me to do now?"

Luther and all the Reformers are clear—our context, personality, and skills may shape the work we do but our true vocation always includes prayer, preaching, and sacrificing for our neighbors within that work. Few of us will be rostered leaders (and that is how God wants it). But God calls all of us to vocation in all the places of our lives. Are we praying for the people we encounter? Have we learned to talk and to listen to the people around us about what God is up to? Do our lives sacrificially reflect the impact of Christ in the midst of our actions and choices? Or do we look like everyone else?

An effective congregation in mission in the twenty-first century will equip people for these basic tasks: It will teach people to pray and help them discover what that means within their life's work. It will help them hear God's story and then equip them to share it in their daily conversations. And it will help people discern what Christ is calling them to do and support them as they make sacrificial choices in their lives. As each of us finds ways to carry out this work in the midst of all we do, not only will we discover our vocation to be useful to God, but lives will be changed and glimpses of God's dream will find their way into our world.

For Reflection and Discussion

1. Martin Luther and John Calvin, to name two, saw Jesus as the one to whom we turn to glimpse a vision of the life God wants for us. Read Philippians 2:5-11. How does Paul see Jesus as a model for our lives? What does he hope happens as a result?

2. As you think about your daily life, who are you called to be praying for on a regular basis?

3. Think about a conversation you had recently with someone you see often. If you shared good news from God in that conversation, how did you do it? If not, what could you have said?

4. Living sacrificially means making choices that put others first. What are the sacrificial things you do with your life and who benefits as a result?

Prayer

Dear God, in Jesus we see a vision of the way we are intended to be. As he was on the cross he prayed for us, shared good news with those around him, and offered his life for us. Help us to care deeply for those around us, to bring them to you in prayer, and to show love for them in word and in deed. We pray in Jesus' name. Amen

5

An Introduction to PAWN Analysis

We have seen that God is on a loving mission to bless, save, heal, reconcile, and set free the whole creation. And God's mission has room for all sorts of allies. But how can we know exactly what we should be doing to help in God's mission? How can we decide where to focus our resources in order to be most effective and useful to God? After all, there are many things each of us could do. But most of us have discovered that, if we try to do *everything*, we end up doing nothing well.

Many people find it helpful to have some framework to gather and organize thoughts in a meaningful way. This can assist anyone to get a clearer sense of where God is calling them to drill down and focus their energy, time, passion, and financial resources for the sake of really getting something *done*. We use a tool called PAWN Analysis to help us see what possibilities lay before us. In a chess game, the pawn is a frontline piece. By itself, it can seem rather ordinary and unimportant. But good chess players know that without them the rest of the set is weak and with them, a variety of things can happen. PAWN analysis can help you make a variety of things happen as you serve on God's front lines as well.

What Is PAWN Analysis?

The Great Commandment (Matt. 22:36-40) reminds us how much *God* values all *people* and calls us to do the same. Jesus tells us that God's real desire goes way beyond religious faithfulness to life faithfulness; God works to make love real in everyone and every-where. We are to love God with everything we've got. We are to love our neighbor as we love ourselves. God's dream is that when the kingdom is here in all its fullness, real relationships, grounded in love, will exist between God and people and between people and people. No one is to be left out. No one is off the hook.

PAWN Analysis is based in this simple scriptural model that recognizes all three parties: God, ourselves, and our neighbors are all involved in God's work and a part of God's dream. It is a tool we use to see how we can begin to think about God's mission and activity in the world—both in a general way and, more specifically, in our own lives and the lives of others. Practically, PAWN Analysis is a tool for seeing what we could actually *do* once our purpose and direction is clear. There are four key parts to PAWN Analysis:

(P) Purpose: This is our role in God's mission. God is up to some-thing, and our purpose helps us stay clear about the part we play. It includes the principles we will practice as we carry out that purpose.

(A) Assets, Gifts, and Passions: These are the good things that God has given to each of us and/or planted in us to use as we carry out our purpose.

(W) Wow!: These are the good things that God is already doing in our lives.

(N) Needs: These are issues we face that require help or added resources.

Using PAWN Analysis, above all, reminds us that our job is to serve the Lord in all things. Like the pawn on a chessboard, we are called to be on the front lines of God's mission to love, bless, save, heal, reconcile, and set free the whole world.

PAWN Analysis

Vision for Action
Options you have to
be useful to God!

Missional Identity
*Purpose - Your role in
God's mission*

Neighbor(s)
A). Assets, gifts and passions
*B). Wow! Good things already
    happening*
C). Needs neighbors have

You
A). Assets, gifts, and passions
*B). Wow! Good things already
    happening*
C). Needs you have

The PAWN Analysis diagram has three arrows pointing inward. One is for our purpose, which is defined by our part in God's mission to bless and save our world. We include principles in this area as well. These help us not only define what our purpose is but also the values and behaviors we will use as we pursue that purpose. A second arrow is for our context, the neighbors whom God has given us to relate to and partner with. It includes viewing our neighbors not only as objects of mission but also as partners on the journey as we await the coming of God's kingdom and work to be involved in it. And the third arrow is for you, a child of God and part of God's people who have been called to be agents for God in the world.

Note that *both* the you and your neighbor share a lot of similarities—both have assets, gifts, and passions; both have needs; and both have wows—those places and things where God is already at work. In fact, there may only be one key difference between you and your neighbor—how you view your role in God's work. We believe we know a bit about what God is up to because of what God has done in Jesus and to what God continues to call us through the work of the Holy Spirit. In other words, the main difference between the church and the world is our sense of *purpose*. But God is on the loose and at work everywhere—in the church and in the world.

Knowing what to *do*, for Christians, comes from *being* who God has created us to be through our assets, wows, and needs and being able to *see* what God is *already doing* so that we can be a part of it! Notice that the fourth arrow—a vision for action—comes *out* from the center. As we see the assets, wows, and needs in our lives and in the lives of others around us, new ideas for action emerge. Best of all, each of these actions is possible because it springs out of the very real resources God has already given us!

Many church leaders are finding PAWN Analysis to be a useful tool, but this same model could be used on the job, at home, and in our neighborhoods. God is on the loose and already at work in all those places and beyond. We just need eyes to see and a desire to join in. Using this model gives us a simple way to organize our thoughts and see new ways to make a real difference.

In the next few chapters we will unpack the PAWN Analysis and walk through defining purpose and principles, taking inventory of assets, gifts, and passions, exploring the good things that are already happening around us, and seeing what needs to be more effective. We'll also look at how to begin to do some thinking with and about the neighbors around us. We hope you will take the time to consider the issues and the work presented in each chapter. It will give you a framework to think about your own life, the options before you, and the vocation you have to be useful to God!

For Reflection and Discussion

1. Paul often wrote letters to people who were entrusted to do ministry where they were. An example of this can be found in 1 Corinthians 1:4-9. Look up and read the text to see how Paul offered encouragement to his friends and showed confidence that they can do great things. How is this kind of encouragement given to you through your faith community? Where else do you find it?

2. If you really believed that you had what you need, what would you do to change the world?

3. Who has encouraged you to see possibilities and be motivated to do something significant? How have they done that for you? To whom can you offer insight and encouragement?

Prayer
Dear God, daily we are presented with opportunities to make a difference. Help us to recognize the possibilities around us. Help us both to encourage and be encouraged by others—so that all we do might reflect your love for our world. In Jesus' name we pray. Amen

6

"P" Is for Purpose

Have you ever gotten up to do something and in the middle of the task been distracted? You get up from your seat, start off in the right direction, and suddenly realize that whatever it was you were getting ready to do has completely vanished from your mind! All you can do is ask yourself, "All right, why am I here?"

The answer to that question is one of life's fundamental quests. The search for purpose and meaning has inspired philosophers, songwriters and poets, engineers and inventors, and just about every creative or philosophical venture in history. Almost everyone would rather have a life that matters than not. And almost everyone would like to know, "Why am I here?"

The "P" in PAWN Analysis is about our purpose and the principles we embody to live out that purpose. In this chapter we'll look at our purpose; we'll think about our principles in the next.

It is important to remember that we are not talking about personal mission here. There is only one mission, and it belongs to God. God is on a mission to save and bless the world God made and loves, and in Jesus God has promised that mission will be completed. Through Jesus and the power of the Holy Spirit the kingdom of God is breaking in today and one day will come into all its fullness. We don't need to worry about it; it is part of God's promise. The future belongs to God, and God can be trusted.

What we are talking about is how each of us understands our role in God's mission: if God is active and alive in the world in which we live, then what should we be doing in light of that truth and how can that shape us and mold us as we seek to participate in what God is doing around us? Here it is important to recognize that as each of us thinks about our personal purpose, we recognize that we have many roles in our lives. Each of them offers a place and a way for us to be part of what God is doing, but none of those roles, by itself, is our purpose.

One pastor we worked with asked for help defining purpose and guiding principles for his life. For a while he wrestled with what to think, what to say, and what to claim as his purpose. He read scripture. He prayed. He reflected. For a while nothing seemed to click, then one day it came together for him. What happened to help him make the shift? He said, "Once I recognized that being a pastor was not my purpose in life, it set me free to find out what was. I think I was blocked by my job—especially since I have always thought that being a pastor was my purpose in life. Once I saw that my purpose came from my baptism and not my ordination, I could think in new ways. Then I could sense my purpose."

He went on to reflect on his various roles in life—husband, father, friend, pastor, individual—and he began to think about what it was that was most important to him that tied all those roles together. He began to think about the way God used him in each of his roles. He began to think about what God was hoping for in his life and the mark he would leave, not just on his parishioners but on all of the people his life touched—and on the world.

We Are More than a Job!

All of us are pressured to define ourselves by our occupations, though it is perhaps more tempting for people in some professions to do that than it is for others. People whose jobs are in religious work or in the helping professions can easily assume that their purpose in life is their work. It is harder to define life by our work when we are less clear about how that work contributes to what God is doing. But the truth is, we can be part of what God is doing to bless the world in *any* occupation. And we should be participating in what God is doing in every aspect of our lives. In some ways, any of us who discover this truth will find ourselves set free to thrive in a new way.

Take for instance, Andy, who works in a factory. On the surface many might think his work was unpurposeful—just a job. But all jobs provide opportunity to produce helpful things; they provide income to help support our families, resources to share with others as part of a generous life, and interactions with others with whom we work. Just that can be a lot! God has little interest in us producing useless things, ignoring our family or our other neighbors' needs, and living in isolation!

Over the last few years Andy has paid more and more attention to how his life contributes to what God is doing in the world. Andy has a deep love of older people, and through his congregation he has volunteered to visit shut-ins and bring them communion. He has the ability to invite others to join him in that passion. Andy also has deep compassion for people who are struggling—something that he sees more and more often in the economic climate facing our country and world as we write this book—and so he cooks and serves. He has a deep love of God, so he keeps a Bible in his truck and he reads it regularly as a part of his work life. And he loves to see others find meaning and usefulness in their lives, so he is open to helping and inviting others to be open as well. In the process of his personal growth as a Christian and as a minister in all he does, Andy has inspired many people to rethink the purpose and meaning of their lives.

Even if we are outside the church institution most of the time, we can be useful to God. Sent to work in the world, like the pawns on a chessboard, the people of God serve as the front lines of God's allies. Paid by the world, most of God's workers find livelihood among the very people and places in which they are sent!

Our sense of purpose is about the *point* of our lives. We all share a common connection to what God has done, is doing, and promises to complete. Those of us who follow Jesus do so out of a common connection and confidence that we are allied with a cause that cannot fail. God's kingdom is coming. In fact, it breaks in, and we can see glimpses of it all the time!

We Are Useful to God!

In spite of the fact that all of us share a common sense of purpose, we believe it is still important for each of us to reflect biblically, prayerfully, and intentionally about our personal sense of purpose. And it is important that this move from putting words on a piece of paper—creating a purpose statement—to something deeper. In Jeremiah, the prophet tells us that God will put the new covenant "in their hearts" (Jer. 32:40). It's more important to own our purpose within our hearts than it is to come up with just the right words to describe it!

Spend some time reflecting on the questions at the end of this chapter. Dig into scripture and think about what you see God doing. Think about the various ways your life crosses the paths of others and what you see God doing in each of these places. Ask others what they see in you and how you have been able to be an agent of God in their lives. And if you are floundering, think ahead to the very end of your life. When it is your turn to leave this world to those who follow you, what would you like people to say about the difference your life made for them? What mark do you see God making and what mark would you like to leave on the world as your part of God's mission?

Right now there is a strong interest in environmental issues, especially related to climate change. We hope it is not just a fad but a real change of heart, with enduring impact on how we all live together on this earth that we all share. One of the common images used to describe the impact we have on the environment is our "carbon footprint." All around us we see signs, ads, magazine and newspaper articles, TV specials, and web pages encouraging us to reduce our carbon footprint. It is a helpful reminder that the way we live has an impact on the earth, whether we are intentional or not. What we do in our lives does make a difference, and unfortunately, our carbon footprint is a measure of how bad our mark on the world can be!

What if we measured our lives by God's footprint? Instead of trying to just minimize the damage we do, what if we tried to maximize the good? Instead of trying to make the earth bleed a little less, what if the things we did brought a smile to God's face more often? What if everywhere we went, people saw signs that God had been there because of the mark our lives have left behind?

We all have a purpose, and while we need to articulate it for ourselves and make sense of it by connecting to the people and places around us, our purpose is more alike than it is unique. In one way or another we all share a common purpose to watch for what God is doing to bring about the kingdom of God on earth and to participate in ways that further the work. We see God enter our world and work among us each and every day, and we join in to share love and participate in what God is doing.

Participation is important when considering our purpose. Often, a crew of people working on something draws spectators. For a while the workers will tolerate having someone watching from the sidelines, but eventually one of them will grab a tool, hand it to the spectator and say, "Here, make yourself useful!" That is essentially what God says to each of us. God comes in Christ, gets involved bringing glimpses of the kingdom all around us as we watch, and then God says, "Here, make yourself useful!" When we take up that invitation, we have reclaimed the "V" word, and life takes on a whole new sense of meaning.

For Reflection and Discussion

1. Read Psalm 1. If you are using this book in a group, consider reading it aloud as a group in unison or responsively. What is

it that the psalmist sees as the source of happiness for people? Where do people find life? How can that help us know where to look for useful and joy filled lives now?

2. Think about the way God is working through you. How would you describe God's action to someone else?

3. Knowing what you know now, complete a draft of the following: "God's purpose for my life is to _____." You will probably want to work to refine and clarify this over time. If you are using this book in a group, discuss your initial drafts with each other.

Prayer

Good and loving God, you have a use for all of us that gives each of our lives purpose and meaning. Help us to sense you using us and to be clear that you have made us to be your agents in the world, loving and serving our neighbors. In Jesus' name we pray. Amen

7

"P" Is for Principles

Claiming a sense of purpose for our part in God's mission can serve as a pointer for our lives—in fact, it is *the point* of our lives. The willingness to own our purpose and to devote ourselves enthusiastically to fulfilling that purpose is the centering, grounding reason we do what we do—whatever and wherever we do it!

Even though the point of our lives is deeply similar, the *plot* of our lives is quite unique. Each of us has a variety of circumstances, settings, and relationships that are unlike the matrix of anyone else's life. How we carry out our individual purpose depends on a number of factors. Some of those factors will be based on personal assets and passions, on the good things God is up to in and through our lives, and on the places where we have needs. Some factors will be based on the things we have in common with the people and places around us.

And so there is a second aspect to the "P" in PAWN. In addition to purpose, we each have values that shape our behaviors and the decisions we make. Having well thought out and articulated principles is remarkably helpful for guiding our thinking and doing, and they serve as a transition to connect the point of our lives to its plot. Shaped by scripture, environment, culture, and our relationship with God and God's people, we can begin to put a stamp on what we do as we live out our stories.

Saying What's Most Important
Principles are often discerned in community. In fact, as authors we have been blessed always to wrestle with guiding principles in

partnership with others. The dialog and ability to discern with and through the voices of others have helped us to shape and be shaped in ways that encourage our work to grow deep roots and find a creative spark. If you can join with people of common commitment with whom you will journey, you may want to do this work in partnership with others as well.

But, we also have seen and helped people work to develop their own personal set of guiding principles. It can be done well and provide depth and meaning for those willing to spend time thinking about what is important to them—people they have admired as ones sent by God, reading scripture, and praying for insight to shape them. At the end of this chapter are some questions to help start this process of discernment, along with ways to help define and refine the work for ourselves.

It helps to think of guiding principles as a way of working with our purpose to shape and customize its work in our lives. If our purpose helps define the direction of our life's journey, the guiding principles help frame the path we will take. Once we have some idea of where we are going, the guiding principles help us shape the way we will choose to get there—a bit like the lines on a road provide the parameters within which we may drive a car, but they don't actually steer the car for us or help us avoid potholes or fill up with gas. They simply frame our journey and keep us operating in a range that helps us stay true to ourselves along the journey.

We have all known people who have had to make decisions in some aspect of their lives where their values were at stake. Someone or something had put them in a place outside their values and they had to make a decision: "Do I do this or not?" The more principled people are, the easier it is to wrestle with these decisions and come out the other side okay.

For example, a young man working for a major brokerage firm was asked to dump a few shares of weak stocks along with some stronger ones into the portfolio of the firm's clients. By mixing the stocks, the company could get rid of the weak ones without customers noticing. This would allow the company to move some shares high and let someone else take the hit low. When asked to do this, the young man immediately felt conflict with his own personal values. While his job paid well and was his primary livelihood, there was no way he could bring himself to go against his values. So he quit his job and cleared out his desk. Awareness of his core values was enough to make the decision easy. Some people might have stayed on (in fact, he was the only one to quit that day), but for him, the guiding principles that shaped his life were too far removed from what he was asked to do. Leaving was an easy choice—even if it didn't mean life would be easy.

It is possible, that without that value conflict, he'd still be working in the same place. But leaving the job, combined with ongoing reflection about what he wanted to do with his life, gave the young man another chance to connect his occupation, his passions and concerns for the world, and his values in a way that took him into the next chapter of his life. Reclaiming the "V" word is about these kinds of moments and the decisions many of us face at key times in our lives. Today, the young man has continued to use the same gifts and talents to raise millions of dollars for nonprofit companies. He has dedicated volunteer energy to support work on college campuses to raise awareness and involvement of college students about world hunger. And he feels that his life is useful and consistent with the values he holds.

Discerning Our Own Guiding Principles

Many of us have our deepest values clearly resting in our core. They have been shaped by key relationships, our upbringing, decisions we have made, and organizations of which we have been a part. For Christians, biblical truths and the teaching of the church have often been strong influences in shaping our core values, and we use what we have almost instinctively. But reclaiming the "V" word is about more than instincts; it is about intentionality. If we were to spend some time thinking about what matters most, identifying those whom we most admire, and articulating what is most important in our decisions and actions—what would we say? Leaf through your Bible to see what pages are worn. Chances are they contain the verses that have given you the most meaning.

We can tell a lot about ourselves from the passages we love. When Dave got married his wife gave him a Bible. Over the years as he read its pages, those that were visited again and again became torn, frayed, and yellowed from use. Eventually the spine of the Bible split at the place he visited most often—Jesus' Sermon on the Mount in Matthew 5–7. It is no coincidence that verses from those texts are included in his funeral instructions for use when he dies. In Matthew 6 we read how Jesus gave examples of flowers dressed in a splendor greater than Solomon's finest and pointed out birds flying free and living well fed without working for food. According to Jesus, the flowers and birds are examples of what a life of complete trust looks like. There is freedom without worry, full engagement with the present moment. "Do not worry about tomorrow," Jesus said, "for tomorrow will bring worries of its own. Today's trouble is enough for today" (Matt. 6:34).

Another way to reflect on what we value most is to think about our physical possessions. Suppose God were to come one night in a vision and say, "You have too much stuff! Tomorrow night your house will burn down. Everyone will get out. No one will be hurt. But you can bring only five things with you before it happens." What would we bring and why? Like many North Americans, we probably do have too much stuff. And while much of it is useful, little of it holds any real long-term emotional value. What are the few things that do and what can we learn about ourselves from them?

Those of us who are willing to spend the time reflecting can eventually focus in on five to seven things that are most important in the shaping of our lives. Worded as "I" statements, these things can help communicate to others who we are and help remind us of our values as we live and carry out our roles in God's work. Following are some questions to think about as you pray, study, and reflect on your personal identity and your principles. We hope it is a chance for God to affirm what is best about who you already are and also to discover or articulate some new insights for the journey ahead.

For Reflection and Discussion

1. Read Romans 12:1-2. From where does Paul think our values are to come? How does he see us understanding and clarifying them? What difference are these to make as we live our lives?

2. Reflect on biblical characters that you admire. What attracts you to them? List those characteristics on a sheet of paper. Then think about a few of your heroes and role models—they can be as close as family or as distant as famous people you admire. What do you admire about them? Add those characteristics to your list.

3. List five to seven things you want to be true for your life, using the format, "I (verb)," for example, "I give generously of who I am." Use these statements as a *first draft* of your own personal guiding principles. If you are using this book in a group, share your observations to these questions. There should be lots to talk about!

Prayer

Dear God, you mold us and shape us as we journey through life. We thank you for the movement of your Holy Spirit, the ministry of Jesus, and the modeling and care that we have received from others who are examples to us in life. Help us to reflect on what is important and to claim those things as guiding principles for our own lives. In Jesus' name we pray. Amen

8

Assets, Wows, and Needs in You

We know God has a purpose for us all and in large part it is the same for each of us. God is on a mission to love and bless and reconcile all of creation, and because of who God is and how God works, we have a purpose. God does not wave a magic wand to make it all happen; instead, as scripture points out, God engages us in this work and calls us to participate. Since the beginning, God's people have had a similar purpose to be a part of what God is up to wherever we find ourselves.

So, if the *point* of our stories has a common theme, what makes us all different is the *plot* of our stories. We each have been blessed with different assets, gifts, and passions. We find ourselves surrounded by different events happening in our homes, our offices, and our communities. If we take a look at what's happening in our lives, we will see that some things make God smile and some, well, not so much!

Let's look at those scripture stories again. God told Abraham to walk the land, looking as far as he could to the East, to the West, to the North, and to the South, to see the extent of God's blessing and to realize how he and Sarah could be a blessing to others. When Jesus called the disciples, he invited them to use the skills and mindset they had to do a new thing—fish for people. And it is easy to forget that Paul traveled from town to town, making tents, getting to know people, and starting churches everywhere he went. It was his trade as a tent maker, not a teacher of the Law, that put him in a position to have conversations with people and allowed him to share the word about Jesus and usher in a new day. God used his gifts to change the world.

Assets, Gifts, and Passions

So what's your story? At workshops around the country we ask folks what it means to be a missionary in their everyday lives. Working in teams, we help them to imagine what that looks like in their corner of the world. As they get to know one another, team members ask each other about what makes them tick. Where have they been in school, in work, in geographic location—well, in life? What do they bring to the table? What gets their hearts pumping or keeps them up at night because they can't stop thinking about it? These are the kinds of questions that begin to get at what are our assets and passions.

Personal assets can include a lot of things. Assets may be educational, such as a degree in some profession. Assets may also include volunteer experience that helps a person understand how to motivate people even when they don't receive a paycheck. For example, twenty years of experience in raising a family can help someone understand how to schedule a group of people going in many directions. Hobbies can be assets too. We might see them as personal diversions, but they can be useful when connected to what God is doing in the lives of people. In addition, physical assets—home, vehicles, and personal possessions—allow us to have the material means with which to reclaim our vocations.

Our talents or gifts fall under the heading of assets, too. Some people are natural musicians; others have an affinity for working with numbers. These are gifts! Some of us have the ability to empathize with the hurts and hopes, the dreams and realities of others. This, too, is a gift. But it is not enough to identify our assets and gifts. We need to use them! Education and work experience are definitely assets, but only when we recognize how they can be useful to God at the moment. For instance, someone gifted in technology with a talent for easily making friends with new people could hang out with some seniors at the library, teaching them how to get online to talk to their grandchildren and great grandchildren. Using our gifts and passions in this way can make a real difference!

Tana loves making things beautiful. It led her to a first career in design and cosmetology. And although she has moved on to other work, she still loves helping make things that are just ideas—dreams in the making—become new realities. In fact, she uses this passion in a new way in her current job all the time. How do we identify our passions? It helps to think about the things that engage us and seem to make time fly, or that make us feel more energized when we're done than when we started. What makes us smile and laugh most often? Where do we love spending time? What is it we like to do when we are avoiding our "to-do" lists? These are our passions!

Wows!

So many times we stop following a dream or a passion because we feel as if we have to start from scratch—and that just doesn't seem like a realistic possibility. We tell ourselves, "I'm too old. I don't have enough time to start that kind of project. I already have too many letters after my name. Going back to school is just not an option." But often, we don't need to start a new thing to find meaning or purpose in our lives. Often, we already possess what's needed, and to get moving we just need to tap into the momentum that's already there.

That's where wows can help. Wows are places in our lives where things are already happening, where God is already up to something significant. For some people, that could mean becoming involved in a neat, new program in a professional organization they've been a part of forever. Others might look to their local sports organization, the one their kids have participated in every week for the last ten years. They know everyone from the endless hours on the soccer field but have never really tapped into the friendships beyond killing time each and every Saturday. Now is the time. Or it could be the hundreds of friends we have connected with on Facebook who are dying to know what we are up to each and every minute of the day. A wow may simply be taking advantage of our usual lunch crowd, connecting with someone who has experience in the new thing we want to try! It's as simple as asking ouselves, "Who do I know? What neat things am I already a part of that is just waiting for me to join in?"

Since wows are the good things that are already happening, they can help us start with momentum. And it is always easier (and more fun) to start in a place where things are moving. That's what wows can do!

Needs

Needs are critical to our ability to get anywhere. They call us to another place. Our needs are part of what drives us to learning and experiencing life. In our workshops we often teach the change formula. It goes like this:

Dissatisfaction x Vision x Action Steps > Cost of Change

We won't go into this whole formula for change right here, but note that it is a multiplication formula. If anything in the formula is zero, the whole thing goes to zero. This means we have to have things with which we are dissatisfied in order to make a move. We have to have some discomfort with the way things are. If we don't then we are just stuck right where we are.

Sometimes our needs are the very thing that makes us uncomfortable enough to make a change. When Tana's family moved to Chicago a few years ago they bought a condo in the heart of the city. At the time they thought their youngest, a son, would be living with them part time. Their middle and oldest daughters were going to be away at college. Their needs for a large place were not very great. Little did they know that within a short period of time their son would be living there full time and both girls would be within walking distance! Suddenly, they found themselves with five adults in and out of the house on a regular basis. Plus, there often would be added friends. To complicate things further, their condo had to hold their offices, living space, and some teen play/relaxing space—you get the picture!

As the stress of the living situation increased, everyone felt the pressure. Because their son's bedroom was small, Tana and her partner made the TV area more available for him to relax in. This was great for the son, but it created a new problem for the parents, since a room gained for the kids meant a room lost for the adults. And since the office and the living room were in the same space, they were left with two choices: go to bed or work. There was no place to play, enjoy time with friends, read, or watch an occasional movie. It got to the point where Tana didn't like being in her own home! Her needs had gotten to the breaking point. It wasn't until the discomfort was so great that they began to develop a vision for a way of living that gave them everything they needed. They planned for teen space, workspace, eating space, and space for quiet down time. With some creativity they carved out a whole new living space, arranging the furniture in a way that kept it separate from their desks and work. And once the changes were made, all kinds of activities and people have their own space these days. The result—life is better!

But remember, needs are not just limited to discomfort or dissatisfaction. They can be realities in who we are and how we function. We meet all sorts of people who learn in different ways. They each need certain things to learn the best. Some people need to be with other people to be energized for the task at hand. Others need space and time alone. Some require a list to stay on course. Some are very detailed while others need an accountability partner so they aren't chasing every shiny object that comes along. Many people might find it be helpful to have a coach to assist them achieving a new move that engages assets, gifts, and passion—someone who can help them network to make the most of their wows. It's time to stop looking at needs as deficiencies and start looking at them as growing edges that can help us live into the very thing for which we were created!

Turning to Neighbors

Having a good handle on the assets, wows, and needs in life is an essential part of discovering how we can be most useful to God. Because God wants to use who we are, the better we understand ourselves, the more we will have at our disposal to make a real difference and help impact the world God loves. At the end of this chapter are several questions to help take inventory of what you have to work with. Take some time to reflect on the questions and how they help shed light on the person you are.

We have one last place to look—to the people around us. Not only do we bring things to the table, but our neighbors bring a lot of things into the picture as well. And if our lives are going to take on real meaning, it will be in partnership with our neighbors. In fact, as we have seen earlier in this book, all of this only makes sense when it includes our neighbors. So to fully see how our vocation can be most useful to God, we will turn in the next chapter to our neighbors to see how where we live and who is around us can help us discover a vision for our lives.

For Reflection and Discussion

1. Read 1 Corinthians 12:1-14. How does Paul see gifts being distributed? Who gets them? How do you think about your own gifts and where they come from?

2. Consider your personal assets, gifts, and passions. Think about the things you have to at your disposal. List your assets. List your

gifts and talents. List your passions—the things you care most deeply about.

3. Take into account your wows. What are the good things that God is *already* using you to do? How might others say God is using you right now?

4. What do you need to move ahead? Needs could include personal support, training, or something tangible. Write down your needs. If you are using this book in a group, this is a great chance to do some "homework" on all the above questions and then come back together next time to share your observations!

Prayer
Generous God, you have given us much to work with and you provide for our needs. Help us to use what you have already given us and to appreciate the amazing things you are doing in our lives. In Jesus' name we pray. Amen

9

Assets, Wows, and Needs in Our Communities

Chicago's South Loop is a pretty interesting place. It is just south of the major business district in the heart of the city. Not too long ago—in the early 1990s—there wasn't much there. Tours would come through the area previously known for speakeasies, brothels, and bootleggers and see little more than parking lots and a few sprinkled buildings that formerly were warehouse space.

But today as you travel this area you are surrounded by college and university campuses, residential high-rise buildings, restaurants, and a myriad of retail stores, from your mom and pop variety to your local Home Depot. Schools and tennis courts, coffee shops, dog parks, and museums line the lakefront. You can feel the energy, especially in the summer as people make their way to ride their bikes along the shores of Lake Michigan or head to concerts in Grant or Millennium Parks. One is never at a loss for something to do, a new idea to try, or an event to take in.

It's hard not to see God at work as the trees change their color or as the lake sparkles with the morning sun shining on it. God's creative hand is at work as new art work is installed in park land once just green with grass, now alive with the movement of giant legs and torsos. You can see God in the new friendships that take form at the dog park or over a cold beer at the local outdoor café. You can feel it as people pick out their Christmas tree on a local open lot and walk it home to decorate while enjoying the warmth of a hot coffee. You see a mix of people from all walks of life, families formed in virtually all combinations of race, sexual orientation, and religions.

But this is only part of the picture of this neighborhood. In this area you will also find the Pacific Garden Mission, a homeless shelter for men. There are buildings boarded up waiting for a gentle hand and a dream. As you walk down the street, chances are you will find a very well appointed man on his favorite corner selling *StreetWise*, the local paper of the homeless, written and sold by those who live on the streets. Walk a little farther and you will come across buildings in development that yesterday looked like promise and today more like the uncertainty of an economy that is sorely shaken.

Like the South Loop, the communities in which we live are important to God and God is at work in them. Our neighborhoods, workplaces, and homes all have assets, wows, and needs. Have you looked lately? Did you see the bustle of activity in the parks last night? What did you see written on the signs and billboards that you drove by going to work this morning? How about the trash that hasn't made it into the corner garbage can, or the graffiti spray painted on the side of the corner building? Maybe you caught a glimpse of the teens hanging out and smoking, looking more like what your mom used to call hoodlums instead of the future of your community. Did you see the bulletin board at your local coffee shop with all of the papers encouraging you to check out the poetry reading on Friday night or the mom-and-tot playgroup on Thursday afternoon? All of these things are important.

It is not enough to just look at our own assets, wows, and needs. Who we are needs to find space in the places we find ourselves. Not only do we need to know who we are and see what we have. We need to look at our neighbors and at our neighborhoods and make connections so that we can do what matters. And it may be that to do that, we *need* our neighbors and their involvement in our lives.

Assets, Gifts, and Passions

In the last chapter we asked, "What's your story?" Here we'll be looking at our neighbor's story. This may mean people in our communities, our families, our workplaces, and anywhere we encounter people that Jesus would have us call "neighbor."

The story of Paul preaching in Athens is a great illustration of how someone can use his or her own assets, wows, and needs and do a good job connecting them with the realities they find in their context. The story starts in Acts 17:16 and goes to the end of the chapter. (It would be helpful to read the account from the Bible!)

As we read the story, we see that Paul was in Athens, spending a good amount of time in the town square, a place where many philosophers engaged in public debate. It was here that he spoke to the public every day. At first, Paul was really upset by all of the idols he found in the city. But a second glance revealed an asset for Paul when he discovered an idol to the "unknown" god. This was just the connection that he needed, and the situation was perfect since there was already a debating arena with an opening for conversation! And so Paul preached and debated until he got himself hauled in to account for himself.

Our first reaction might have been, "What a mess!" But Paul had other ideas. He knew this was his opportunity. Those idols had become an asset for him, and they represented a need in the community. When the council said, "You are saying some pretty startling things. Explain yourself," Paul responded, "Athenians, I see that you are very religious with all those gods out there. I saw one that gave me a moment's pause. That statue to the unknown god, I would like to tell you a little about that One!" The people Paul was talking to had no idea they were worshiping *God*. It took Paul naming God when he saw the opportunity so that others could see it too.

One of the gifts and passions of the community of Elgin, Illinois, is the arts. There is a community auditorium where on many nights you can find orchestra performances, concerts, plays, and the like. During intermission people mingle over a beverage in the lobby, conversing about their day or the show. With its passion for the arts, this community is willing to see things from a variety of perspectives, to be pushed a little by a new movement of music or a new form of dance. Here's what Christopher Kennedy, a major real estate businessman and art lover, has to say about art and our communities:

> We see contemporary art in particular as a civic duty and believe that art has a tremendous capacity to help shape the way people in the city, the community, respond to issues. Contemporary art is not easy or intuitive or accessible to most people. It's hard. It takes work. You need to be open to very different ideas. A big city and culture faces these exact same issues. If Chicagoans are open to contemporary art, then they'll be open to new ideas. If they are open to new ideas, the city will continue to thrive. If the city continues to thrive, the art business does well. So in a sense, contemporary art is good for society, good for the country.[1]

In Paul's day there were debates in the public square. Today we have a variety of places to gather—in parks and stores and museums in cities, in schools and senior centers in rural communities and small towns, in virtual communities that link people across geography using the World Wide Web. God has given us access to these assets, as well as the gifts and passions of our neighbors who use them, in order to connect with people and to name God when we see God working in our midst. We need only to look around our communities to discover the assets contained there.

A final word concerning neighbors' assets, gifts, and passions: as we look around at all the things we have to work with in our context, think about the list of wows created in the last chapter. It may be that if God is at work, we'll see something or someone whom we can invite to help make what God is doing through us even more amazing. Our wows are chances for our neighbors to join us in ways that may help us all to discover a meaningful life in a new way.

Wows!

If the wows in our personal life are all those things we are connected to but have yet to leverage in a new way, then the wows in our community are things we have yet to connect to. When we look at our communities, we should look for instances where God is already at work. And as we consider our assets, gifts, and passions, we need to keep in mind what is already happening in our communities. There is no need to start from scratch. Where is movement already happening?

Lots of times when people move into a new community, they feel disconnected, with a need to make new friends. Almost instinctively, this is a time when people look around for wows—the good things that are already going on around them in this new place. In fact, if we could stay as open and curious about our surroundings as we often are when we first move in, life would take on a new vibrancy more often.

A woman we know moved into the downtown Chicago area. After getting a little bit settled, she knew it was time to start meeting people and engaginge in her community. Where to start? Well, she loves to read. So she got online and Googled book clubs. She found one for professional women over the age of thirty-five who work downtown. It meets in a local wine bar. She found her niche. A variety of books are read with each month's selection chosen by someone in the group. There is great conversation as they wrestle with difficult topics. The group wonders about what it means to be people in this time and place. They challenge each other's understandings and give each other space to find their way. This has been a wow. The woman didn't have to start a group; it was a good thing already up and running.

In the process she gets to stretch her mind and spirit. She gets to learn from the others in the group and be shaped by them. She is challenged by the urban planner who rides her bike to work and inspired by the lawyer whose husband has MS but is currently doing pro bono work and burning the midnight oil working with the Illinois Reform Commission to help end corruption in state government. Not only is this woman challenged by the life stories of the other women in the group, she is discovering opportunities to make a difference.

Most communities have lots of good things already happening. Some are led by local churches and the people who are a part of them. Many others are being done by people unconnected to those faith communities—people who are doing great things from other perspectives and motivated by other things. Part of using PAWN Analysis is not just being open to how we can help others. It is also recognizing that the work of others is useful in God's economy, too. It may be that we don't need to recruit people to start something new. It may mean joining an existing group and helping do what they have already started!

An interesting reality—the wow that God is up to already in someone else's life is often the place where we can put *our* assets to work right away. So watch for your neighbor's wows, especially the ones that you find match your passions and excite you. They may be the easiest place to do something really significant and to get started right away!

Needs

Identifying the needs of our communities may at first seem easy. Unfortunately it is also one of the easiest areas to which we can become blinded. Needs can be things that we pass by each day without realizing them—local headlines and global issues that impact our communities, such as immigration or the economy or the enviroment. As we read the paper or overhear conversations at the coffee shop, what is breaking God's heart?

At a recent workshop with a number of congregations, we asked participants to bring papers from their communities to use in a group activity. In their groups we had them skim different sections of the paper, putting smiley faces wherever they think God is smiling and frowns where they think God's heart is breaking. After they were done we had each group share what they found.

On this particular day one group was more animated and louder than the rest. They were really energized and sounded surprised by what they were finding. During the sharing time, they told us how surprised they were about the many ways God was at work in their community—even the obituaries they read contained information about the lives of people they wished they had known! Then they began to talk about what was breaking God's heart. They told us about a fire that had burned down a playground just around the corner from where their congregation was located. They talked about how sad they were that although many had been to worship since the fire, they had no idea it had even happened. They were upset by their lack of connection with the very community of which they were a part, but they were also energized by the possibilities. The result? They are beginning a new chapter in the plot of their lives, connected to each other, connected to God through God's purpose for them, and connected to their community through a simple need for a new playground.

This is how it worked for one congregation, but it is how it can work for us too—and not just in our communities, but in our workplaces and in our families. What are you hearing in the lunchroom or by water cooler? Are you settling for the typical "How are you? I am fine." greeting or is there something more that you are ready to find, if only you dig a little deeper? Where can connections be made?

A friend of ours at a local university had led trips of college students to Central Mexico for a few years. Her passion for students and for those in need came together in every trip. A few years ago she felt a pull in a new direction. On her last trip to San Miguel de Allende she began asking the women in town about their needs. The answers were quick in coming and all along the same lines: "We need someplace where we know our children are being taken care of so that we can work to keep our families together."

Donna was moved by their response and did what few people have the courage to do. She sold everything she had and moved to Mexico! She started Casa de los Angeles, a free day care center for children in the community that also offers English classes so the parents can get better paying jobs. The mothers and fathers volunteer each week at the center as a way to "pay" for the amazing care their children receive. College students from the United States volunteer to work there—an asset of Donna's previous occupation! Each day of the year people work with the kids, singing songs, finger painting, changing diapers and lives. Donna's assets, gifts, and passions are used every day in new and exciting ways. The assets and passions of others are included in the work. The community's needs are being met through amazing people.

Not every story is so dramatic, but the needs we encounter are real. We don't need to move to another country to meet the needs around us. And none of the needs we find are too small or too large for the people God has created us to be. Dare to look. Dare to dream. And then dare to dive in!

For Reflection and Discussion

1. Read 1 Corinthians 12:12-26. In this lesson we see not only the gifts of one person but the gifts of many being connected together. Why was this important to Paul? How does this change the way you see your co-workers, family members, or neighbors?

2. As you talk with people and observe the setting, what assets and gifts do people have that they could use to make a difference?

What passions do they have—what do they care most deeply about? Make a list. Since these questions are about your neighbors, you may need to make a decision about *which* neighbors you want to consider. With multiple arenas in your life—home, church, occupation, public/community life—you can actually work on these questions over and over in different settings!

3. What are the good things—the wows—that are already happening in your community? What is God smiling about? Where are glimpses of God's dream apparent in your community? Make a list.

4. What needs, shortcomings, or struggles do you see in your community? What are the things that are breaking God's heart? Write these on your sheet as well. If you are working through this book in a group setting, pick a common context (for example—everyone think about your neighborhood or shared workplace together). Discuss and share what you found. You may want to even combine your lists if you are all thinking about the same place!

Prayer
God of creation, you have made all people and places and have given what we need to see possibilities and to see you at work. Give us eyes and hearts that are open to seeing all that is around us as you see it. In Jesus' name we pray. Amen

10

The "V" Word—Discerning Life's Vocation

Throughout this book we have talked about many things related to reclaiming our vocation and living with more intentionality and purpose. In this last section we'll review all the pieces and try to put them together as a whole.

The first piece is to remember is that we are useful to God! No matter what we do or where we do it, we are called by God to be part of God's loving action in the world.

Second, within that calling are common threads that permeate all of our vocations. We are called to stay connected to God in prayer, to tell others of God's commitment to love the world, and to live a sacrificial and servant life—all on behalf of our neighbor. In a sense, vocation is about staying connected to God and living out that connection in word and deed, always serving as the hands, feet, and voice of Christ in the world. The call to carry on the mission of Jesus as a vehicle to love the world is the point of all our stories.

But while the point of all of our stories is similar, the plot of our lives can look very different. To see specifically how this plot takes shape in our lives, we've used PAWN Analysis, examining the purpose, assets, wows, and needs that make up each individual. When we bring together our personal assets, gifts, and passions, along with our wows and our needs, we can begin to piece together our story. Add to that our purpose and we flesh out the plot. Finally, with the addition of the assets, gifts, and passions plus the wows and needs of our neighbors and communities, we unveil a complete vision for the plot of our stories. When we hold on to our purpose and have a clear picture of our assets, wows, and needs, we have a lens through which to focus on our homes, our communities, and our workplaces. With that comes a beautiful new story, one for which God has created us.

Jenn is a new teammate with us. She has multiple degrees in music and the arts, and for a long time she found herself working for various congregations helping people enjoy the arts in worship. She formed and directed choirs, created banners for the worship space, and spent time with children's music especially around the holidays. As things happened, this past year she found she had a bunch of time on her hands. Jenn used the extra time as an opportunity to satisfy her need to work with positive people, and she spent the last several months of the year volunteering for a major political campaign. She directed people in a whole new way. In the process she experienced new ways to use her gifts and assets and the purpose for her life to be a part of a change that as it turns out will affect the whole country! And now, changed by that experience, she is finding a way to make a difference in the Kansas City schools by taking on a role as an organizer to get more adults involved in mentoring and encouraging kids in one of the biggest school districts in the country.

Jenn has remained clear about her purpose to use her artistic gifts to servce God in whatever form it will take. In her new role, she is experiencing ways to see people as they play their various parts, just like on a sheet of music, so that she can facilitate processes where everyone's gifts are engaged. She is conducting in this new context in ways she probably could not have imagined just eight months ago. She is writing a new chapter in her story as she continues to engage who she is with what God is doing in her life.

The questions at the end of each chapter in this book have provided us with the tools to put together an inventory of all sorts of things about ourselves and the world around us. Now we need to spend time putting the pieces together, playing with options, and thinking and praying about the possibilities. It may be that some people will keep doing what they are already doing right in the same place. But like the woman at the well who met Jesus in John 4 and then went into town to reconnect with her neighbors in a new way (right where she was!), these people may also go back to the old place with a new spirit. Rediscovering what God calls us to do brings about a new spirit and energy that changes how we live our lives. We start praying for coworkers, live more sacrificially for others, and find ways to speak words of hope from God in the midst of it all. And we rethink how to live in ways that make better use of who we really are—using our assets, building on the good things in place, and fulfilling more of the needs we have. Once we discover that vocation is simply to be useful to God, we will also find that we have the chance to be freed for new things right where we already are!

Others may decide that the theme of their lives is calling them to make a big change. It may be time to get up and move (like Abraham and Sarah). They may head back to school for more training or change jobs or take on new challenges and connect in new ways with others around them. The authors of this book are working together in a company they helped start—one that has only existed for a little over a year. And the excitement of that venture has already meant new connections, new opportunities, and new skills for all of us.

One last reminder, the elements in this book are not a checklist to use once to find ourselves and then move on. They are all basic to life itself. Over the course of the coming years we may find all sorts of things to occupy our time and energy. Some will involve pay and the world will think of them as a job. Some will not. But in all things our vocation is to be useful to God. And everything we do will be a chance to show love for our neighbor. There will never be a time when we will not be called to pray for people, speak for God, and live sacrificially for the sake of others. And we will always have assets and passions at our disposal, good things happening all around us, and needs to be met. And so will all the people around us.

Are you clear about the *point* of your life? How is the *plot* of your life shaping up? What new chapter is dying to be written? African American theologian Dr. Howard Thurman once said, "Ask yourself what makes you come alive, and then go do that. Because what the world needs is people who have come alive."[1] What are you waiting for? This is your time!

For Reflection and Discussion

1. Read Micah 6:8. If this is how God wants our lives to be, what would it look like for you to live this way? How is it already happening? What would need to change?

2. With the passions you have, how can your assets and gifts be put to good use? How can the assets, gifts and passions of others you know be joined to do something even more significant?

3. As you see needs in the world around you, where do your assets and passions connect in ways where you could do something to help? Where do your passions connect with the deepest needs around you?

4. Think about your wows. What is God doing that you should celebrate and lift up—both in you and in others around you? How can you and others join in with this good stuff?

5. Look back at the various lists and work you did in previous chapters. Think about your purpose and principles as you look at all your options. How does thinking this way help you see your life and the opportunities that are before you, not only now, but in the

future? How could you use the tools in this book to help someone else gain clarity in their life about how to be useful to God right now?

Prayer

Dear God, you have called us in baptism, joined us to the work of Jesus, and given us all we need to be helpful in your mission to bless, love, and save your world. Help us to be clearer about the opportunities before us and bold in our pursuit of the choices we have. May all we do help us and others to see you at work as you build your dream in and through us right before our eyes! In Jesus' name we pray. Amen

Notes

Chapter One

1. Rick Warren, *The Purpose Driven Life* (Grand Rapids, Mich.: Zondervan, 1995).

2. Parker Palmer, *To Know As We Are Known* (New York: HarperOne, 1993).

Chapter Two

1. Dave Daubert, *Living Lutheran: Renewing Your Congregation* (Minneapolis: Augsburg Fortress, 2007).

2. Kelly Fryer, *Reclaiming the "E" Word: Waking Up to Our Evangelical Identity* (Minneapolis: Augsburg Fortress, 2008).

3. Dietrich Bonhoeffer, "Letter to Karl-Friedrick Bonhoeffer on the 14th of January, 1935" in *Testament to Freedom: The Essential Writings of Dietrich Bonhoeffer* (New York: HarperCollins, 1995), 424.

4. "Affirmation of Baptism" in *Evangelical Lutheran Worship* (Minneapolis: Augsburg Fortress, 2006), 236.

Chapter Four

1. Martin Luther, "Sermons on 1 Peter," in *Luther's Works, Vol. 30* (St. Louis: Concordia, 1967), 63.

2. John Calvin, *Commentary on a Harmony of the Evangelists, Matthew, Mark and Luke,* 1555. Vol. 2 (Edinburgh: Calvin Translation Society, 1845), 143. Full edition available online at http://www.archive.org/details/harmonyrevelatio02calvuoft

3. Luther, "Sermons on 1 Peter," 53-54.

Chapter Nine

1. Mary Ellen Sullivan, "Chris Kennedy on Art Fairs and Civic Duty," *Artinfo* (Louise Blouin Media, 2009). Accessed at http://www.artinfo.com/news/story/27433/chris-kennedy-on-art-fairs-and-civic-duty/?printer_friendly=1.

Chapter Ten

1. Larry Chang, comp., *Wisdom for the Soul of Black Folk* (Washington, D.C.: Gnosophia Publishers, 2007), 365.

For Further Reading

Daubert, Dave. *Living Lutheran: Renewing Your Congregation.* Minneapolis: Augsburg Fortress, 2007.

Fryer, Kelly A. *Reclaiming the "E" Word: Waking Up to Our Evangelical Identity.* Minneapolis: Augsburg Fortress, 2008.

Nunn, Michelle, editor. *Be the Change: Change the World, Change Yourself.* Atlanta: Hundreds of Heads Books LLC, 2006.

Palmer, Parker J. *To Know as We Are Known: Education as a Spiritual Journey.* New York: HarperOne, 1993.

Pink, Daniel H. *A Whole New Mind: Why Right-Brainers Will Rule the Future.* New York: Penguin Group (USA): The Berkley Publishing Group, 2006.

Smith, Douglas K. *On Value and Values: Thinking Differently about We in an Age of Me.* Upper Saddle River, N.J.: Prentice Hall: FT Press, 2004.